W9-ANP-623

1969
VIETNAM WAR
PROTEST MARCH

PR0TEST!
March for **CHANGE**

CLERGY

AMERICAN FRIENDS SERVICE COMMITTEE
QUAKER SERVICE 52 YEARS

END W
END POVERTY
AMERICAN FRIENDS
SERVICE COMMITTEE

by Joyce Markovics

CHERRY LAKE PRESS

Published in the United States of America by Cherry Lake Publishing Group
Ann Arbor, Michigan
www.cherrylakepublishing.com

Reading Adviser: Marla Conn, MS Ed., Literacy specialist, Read-Ability, Inc.
Content Adviser: Emilye Crosby, PhD
Book Designer: Ed Morgan

Photo Credits: © Associated Press, cover and title page; © Henry Burroughs/Associated Press, 4; © Associated Press, 5 top; © Harvepino/Shutterstock, 5 bottom; © Associated Press, 6; © Associated Press, 7; Wikimedia Commons, 8; © Claudine Van Massenhove/Shutterstock, 9 left; Wikimedia Commons, 9 right; © Eduardo Francisco Vazquez Murillo/flickr.com, 10; Wikimedia Commons, 11; Wikimedia Commons, 12 top; Wikimedia Commons, 12 bottom; Wikimedia Commons, 13; Wikimedia Commons, 14; © Associated Press, 15; Courtesy of Library of Congress, 16; © Associated Press, 17; Wikimedia Commons, 18 top; © Associated Press, 18 bottom; © Associated Press, 19; © Brandon Bourdages/Shutterstock, 20–21.

Cherry Lake Press is an imprint of Cherry Lake Publishing Group.

Library of Congress Cataloging-in-Publication Data

Names: Markovics, Joyce L., author.
Title: 1969 Vietnam War protest march / by Joyce Markovics.
Description: Ann Arbor, Michigan : Cherry Lake Publishing, [2021] | Series:
   Protest! March for change | Includes bibliographical references and
   index. | Audience: Grades 2-3
Identifiers: LCCN 2020038509 (print) | LCCN 2020038510 (ebook) | ISBN
   9781534186316 (hardcover) | ISBN 9781534186392 (paperback) | ISBN
   9781534186477 (pdf) | ISBN 9781534186552 (ebook)
Subjects: LCSH: Vietnam War, 1961-1975—Protest movements—United
   States—Juvenile literature. | Vietnam—History—1945-1975—Juvenile
   literature. | Peace movements—United States—History—20th
   century—Juvenile literature. | United States—Politics and
   government—1963-1969—Juvenile literature. | United States—Politics
   and government—1969-1974—Juvenile literature.
Classification: LCC DS559.62.U6 M33 2021 (print) | LCC DS559.62.U6
   (ebook) | DDC 959.704/31—dc23
LC record available at https://lccn.loc.gov/2020038509
LC ebook record available at https://lccn.loc.gov/2020038510

Printed in the United States of America
Corporate Graphics

C⦰NTENTS

PROTESTS FOR PEACE

It was a windy November day in 1969. A long line of people twisted through the streets of Washington, D.C. They marched silently, holding candles and white cardboard signs that were all the same size.

VIGIL FOR VIETNAM WAR DEAD

TOO MANY PEOPLE HAVE DIED

4

Each sign had a name or place written on it. "Jay Dee Richter." "Joseph Y. Ramirez." "Vinh Linh, North Vietnam." The names belonged to American soldiers killed during the Vietnam War. And the places were Vietnamese villages that had been destroyed in the conflict. The was called the March Against Death.

Around 40,000 people took part in the protest. There were so many candles that President Richard Nixon said he should send helicopters to blow them out.

Vietnam (VEE-et-nahm) is a small country in Southeast Asia. The Vietnam War lasted from 1954 to 1975.

Judy Droz marched at the head of the line. She had traveled from Missouri to honor her husband who died fighting in Vietnam. "I have come to Washington to cry out for liberty, for freedom, for peace," she said.

Judy Droz holds a sign with her dead husband's name on it. The March Against Death started at Arlington National Cemetery and ended at the White House.

The March Against Death was the lead-up to the largest anti-war protest in history. On November 15, 1969, at least 500,000 people poured into the capital. The mood was friendly yet focused. One of the day's speakers asked, "Are you listening, Nixon?" as a **plea** to the U.S. president to end the Vietnam War. The crowd roared their support.

The November 15 marchers sang "All we are saying is give peace a chance" over and over.

7

THE VIETNAM WAR

What led to the Vietnam War? Long before the war, France colonized Vietnam. In 1941, a group called the Viet Minh formed. Led by Ho Chi Minh, the group wanted the Vietnamese to govern themselves. Minh also wanted a government based on communism.

Thống-Chế đã nói : Đại-Pháp khắng khít với thái bình, như dân quê với đất ruộng.

IDEO.-HANOI.

This poster was created by France as a way to mislead and control the Vietnamese people.

The Viet Minh fought the French in an 8-year war beginning in 1946. The group won the war, despite France getting help from the United States. But France still wanted to control Vietnam.

Ho Chi Minh was inspired by the American Revolution to lead his country to independence.

Viet Minh soldiers

Colonialism is when one country takes control of another. Starting in the 1800s, European settlers colonized much of Africa and Asia and mistreated the people of color living there.

In 1954, the peace agreements called for dividing Vietnam into two, North Vietnam and South Vietnam. Ho Chi Minh became the leader of North Vietnam. He and many Vietnamese wanted to reunite the country.

A 1954 map showing North and South Vietnam

Ngo Dinh Diem shaking hands with U.S. president Dwight D. Eisenhower

The leader of South Vietnam, Ngo Dinh Diem, had ties to France. Instead of supporting Minh, who wanted a free and independent Vietnam, the United States helped Diem. Why? The United States supported French colonialism and feared the spread of communism.

Starting in 1957, **guerrilla** fighters known as the National Liberation Front, or Viet Cong, fought Diem's government. The Viet Cong worked with the Viet Minh, which became the North Vietnamese army.

South Vietamese army

North Vietnamese army

Many of the Americans sent to fight in Vietnam were poor and people of color.

In the early 1960s, U.S. troops were sent to Vietnam to help train Diem's army. The idea of a unified, communist Vietnam was becoming more popular among the Vietnamese. In 1964, the United States claimed the North Vietnamese attacked a U.S. warship to **justify** going to war. More U.S. troops were sent to fight.

By 1968, there were over 500,000 U.S. troops fighting in Vietnam. They bombed North Vietnamese cities and villages, killing hundreds of thousands of people. They sprayed Vietnam with Agent Orange, a deadly poison. It killed plants and sickened millions. The Viet Cong also killed many U.S. troops.

U.S. planes dropping bombs on Vietnam

A nurse treating an injured Vietnamese child

Back at home, Americans began protesting the war. Many believed the war was **unjust**. They took to the streets to march for peace. In 1968, women whose husbands and sons were fighting in or had died in Vietnam led an anti-war march in Washington, D.C. Then, in 1969, even bigger **demonstrations** and marches were held there and around the country.

The 1968 women-led anti-Vietnam War march in Washington, D.C.

END THE WAR IN VIETNAM AND SOCIAL CRISIS AT HOME!

Welcome to the JEANNETTE N PEACE PARADE

MARCHON

The biggest anti-war march took place in Washington, D.C., on November 15, 1969. The Vietnam **Moratorium** Committee organized the event. The committee was made up of anti-war **activists**, including Vietnam **veterans**. They called for the immediate **withdrawal** of all U.S. forces from Vietnam.

The Vietnam Moratorium Committee organized many anti-war events.

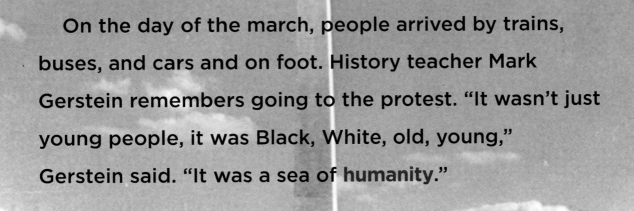

On the day of the march, people arrived by trains, buses, and cars and on foot. History teacher Mark Gerstein remembers going to the protest. "It wasn't just young people, it was Black, White, old, young," Gerstein said. "It was a sea of **humanity**."

Thousands of U.S. soldiers returned home after being badly hurt in Vietnam. Some lost limbs, were **paralyzed**, or had mental problems after seeing people die. Many became powerful anti-war activists.

Activists and musicians addressed the crowd of 500,000. Gerstein remembers Dr. Benjamin Spock speaking about U.S. involvement in Vietnam. "We're not just trying to be policemen of the world, we're trying to control the world," he said.

Dr. Benjamin Spock was a doctor and best-selling author. He strongly believed in ending the war.

Folk singers Peter, Paul, and Mary performed at the march

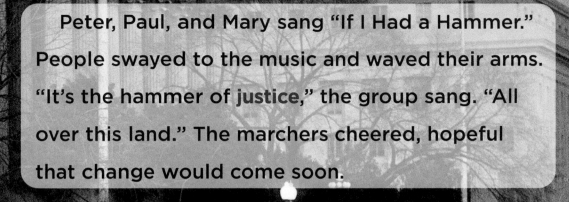

Peter, Paul, and Mary sang "If I Had a Hammer." People swayed to the music and waved their arms. "It's the hammer of justice," the group sang. "All over this land." The marchers cheered, hopeful that change would come soon.

Toward the end of the march, police clashed with protesters. The police used tear gas, which badly burns the eyes, to break up crowds.

The civil rights movement, which tried to end racial discrimination, was a model for the anti-war movement. Many civil rights leaders, like Dr. Martin Luther King Jr., were also anti-war activists.

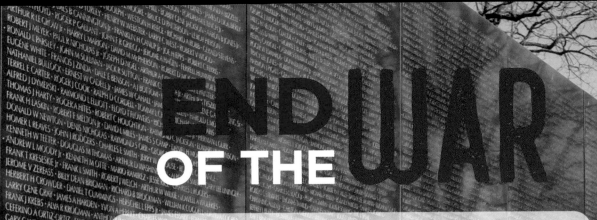

END OF THE WAR

The massive march helped put pressure on President Richard Nixon and U.S. lawmakers. Despite this, the Vietnam War raged on. Finally, in 1973, the United States ended its involvement in the war.

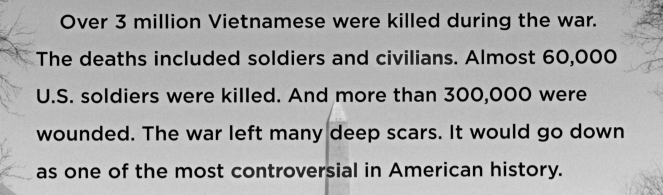

Over 3 million Vietnamese were killed during the war. The deaths included soldiers and civilians. Almost 60,000 U.S. soldiers were killed. And more than 300,000 were wounded. The war left many deep scars. It would go down as one of the most controversial in American history.

The names of the U.S. soldiers who died in the Vietnam War appear on the Vietnam Veterans Memorial in Washington, D.C. The memorial is made up of two 247-foot-long (75 meters) walls.

TIMELINE

1954

May 7
Ho Chi Minh's Viet Minh forces defeat the French.

July
Vietnam splits into North Vietnam and South Vietnam.

1964

August 2 to 4
A supposed attack on a U.S. warship leads to direct U.S. involvement in Vietnam.

1968

January 15
A women-led anti-war march takes place in Washington, D.C.

1969

November 13–15
The March Against Death to end the Vietnam War draws 40,000 people to Washington, D.C.

November 15
At least 500,000 anti-war protesters gather in Washington, D.C.

1973

January
The United States ends its involvement in Vietnam.

1975

April 30
The Vietnam War officially ends.

GLOSSARY

activists (AK-tuh-vists) people who join together to fight for a cause

civilians (suh-VIL-yuhnz) people who are not in the military

communism (KAHM-yuh-niz-uhm) a way of organizing a society in order to divide a country's wealth among the people

conflict (KAHN-flikt) a war or period of fighting

controversial (kahn-truh-VUR-shuhl) causing a lot of argument; not accepted by everyone

demonstrations (dem-uhn-STRAY-shuhnz) public protests against something

discrimination (dis-krim-ih-NAY-shuhn) unfair treatment of others based on differences in such things as skin color, age, or gender

guerrilla (guh-RIL-uh) small groups of fighters who often launch surprise attacks against a larger army

humanity (hyoo-MAN-ih-tee) all people

independent (in-dih-PEN-duhnt) free from the control of others

justice (JUHS-tis) the quality of being fair and good

justify (JUHS-tuh-fye) to explain your actions to try to prove that they are right

moratorium (mor-uh-TOHR-ee-uhm) the stopping or delaying of something

paralyzed (PAR-uh-lized) no longer able to move or feel a part of the body

plea (PLEE) an emotional request

protest (PROH-test) an organized public gathering to influence or change something

unjust (uhn-JUHST) not fair or right

veterans (VET-ur-uhnz) people who have served in the armed forces, especially during a war

withdrawal (with-DRAW-uhl) the action of removing something or ceasing to participate

23

FIND OUT MORE

Books

Henderson, Leah. *Together We March: 25 Protest Movements That Marched into History*. New York: Atheneum Books, 2021.

Hudson, Wade, and Cheryl Willis Hudson, eds. *We Rise, We Resist, We Raise Our Voices*. New York: Crown Books for Young Readers, 2018.

Kluger, Jeffrey. *Raise Your Voice: 12 Protests That Shaped America*. New York: Philomel Books, 2020.

Websites

PBS—Battlefield Vietnam: A Brief History
   https://www.pbs.org/battlefieldvietnam/history/index.html

Time—Why Were Activists 45 Years Ago Protesting "Against Death"?
   https://time.com/3579109/march-against-death

Zinn Education Project—Vietnam War
   https://www.zinnedproject.org/collection/vietnam-war

INDEX

ABOUT THE AUTHOR

Joyce Markovics is a writer and history buff. She loves learning about people and telling their stories. This book is dedicated to all the people who march for a more just future.